W0038343

12 —

*one  wave  standing*

# ONE

# WAVE

# STANDING

---

*William L. Fox*

**LA ALAMEDA PRESS**
**Albuquerque**

Grateful thanks is given to the following editors and their
magazines where some of these poems first appeared:

Natalie Kenvin, *No Røses Review*, "the inland sea"
and "the inland sea, again"

Joe Napora, *Bullhead*, "the island" and "the island, again"

My gratitude is also extended to David Abel, John Brandi,
J.B. Bryan, Gene Frumkin, and Arthur Sze, all of whom
offered advice and friendship to these poems.

ISBN No. 1-888809-06-X
Library of Congress No. 97-078138

All Rights Reserved
First Edition

Copyright 1998 © by William L. Fox

Cover photograph: "Very Large Array"
by Greg Johnston, 1998
Frontis photograph: "Waves of Sand"
by Lehnart & Landrock, 1907

La Alameda Press
9636 Guadalupe Trail NW
Albuquerque, New Mexico 87114

*for*
*Tarn Edward Lyman Fox*
*and*
*Mathew Lyman Fox*

# contents

# *preface*

when i was a child, fog rolled in as waves; the blue whales migrated south and then returned north in waves; i waved goodbye to my mother from the schoolbus as it rolled downhill into the fog toward the ocean.

my bedroom looked north from the hills above town to where desert met the sea, the shoreline white and stubborn, breakers like long lines of prose unreeled from some enormous typewriter over the horizon, their meaning exhausted upon landfall.

father stayed up late night after night in his laboratory by the house, squinting through cigarette smoke at a bank of oscilloscopes, their green faces graphing endless wave forms.

i stood at his side for hours as he adjusted and recalibrated the inputs, waves steepening then flattening out, just like ones at the beach on saturday mornings. he read the standing wave trains and frowned over the decay of information, waved his hands at dials and meters as he tried to explain to me what it all meant.

behind our house the desert stretched east into shadows of the hills. the moon would rise, lightning play far out to sea, and father come out of the lab rubbing his eyes. stretching, he listened for the waves we couldn't hear, then turned to lock up.

years later i stood on a mountain to watch glaciers, and recognized those waves standing in ice at the terminal of collapse, a message i could almost read. still later, my father dead, i moved into the empty quarter of america, only to find the sand dunes and shorelines of the interior crumbling away from comprehension, a text still encoded in waves.

# *transmittal*

## I.

the  wave  stands  on  its  own  //  yet
in  the  long  chain  of  greetings
and  departures  //  transmits  that  which
came  before  //  and  that  which
follows

the  wave  stands  alone  //  yet  locates
itself  before  and  after  //  long  echoes  in
the  standing  train  of  thought  and
speech

wind  rises  upon  water  //  water  upon
the  shore  and  //  what  we  hear  rises
within  a  single  wave  //  the  gray
sea  bearing  vowels  //  before  a
consonant  shore

## II

a voice across the room // the
advance of light in its coherent run
at daybreak // the wave of your
hand to the deepening whistle of the
train // as it pulls away // the light
in your eyes reddening as the
message grows longer // fainter by
any measure

the wave maintains its curvature in
air // a line of clouds along the
mountain chain // spills over the
crest // and it rains // the wave passing
on in the middle atmosphere

the ocean rises and falls with the
weight of sunlight // conversation rising
and falling // raining down on us in
a room a continent away

## III

fortunes rise and fall through a deck
of cards // red aces raining down
upon green felt // wind blowing from
the front of the house out the back
// pages turning one by one next to
the bed // words rising and falling

the wave moves on // carries nothing
to or from us // truth and lies
rising and falling as // the train
departs // a function of the wave //
those on board deaf to the past

underneath the facades of great
buildings // faces rise and fall in the
crowd // columns on the public square
collapsing as // the wave enters the
ground // cornices an avalanche of
dust // red aces raining down.

# the carrier wave
### elbert marr fox

**1944**

in the heavy offshore waters of the north atlantic
the destroyer cuts through twenty-foot waves
its wake a trail of aluminum debris
random reflections you hope will
confuse the enemy radar

you however are not confused
the faces around you camouflaged black
the rubber raft slick and cold the
run to shore through the break in the cliffs
a near miss with
hypothermia and searchlights

you are not confused until
years later on uppers and downers
alcohol and cigarettes you
fumble the wirecutters in your lab
remembering how you cut and stripped
the radar rig off that island while

commandos cut the throats
of the german technicians
stripping them for intelligence

in the heavy cold waves of that war
you leave the island
enter the airwaves to live in code
listening only to what
comes through your headphones

**1958**
starlight breaks on the roof of the lab
and you're still listening outward
up through the huge mutant earphones
and the radio mast to palomar where
photons stream in waves through the open dome
breaking onto the great mirror
light cracking from instrument to instrument
in the code of galaxial behavior

far over the horizon in the wavering night
a heavy cruiser steams west

sonar breaking over an island not yet
risen in the waves and you're listening

while in our house
mother twists a bight of her red hair
waiting for the satellite to orbit into range
you're plugged into it all the way out
to the edge of the known universe

and still the debris of your life
invents confusion the signals crossed the
code indecipherable at such close range
and you miss her leaving
wirecutters helpless to untangle
the device of your love

**1963**
anchored deep in southern new mexico
in the outback of australia and on
an island in mid-ocean
the upended radio telescopes
listen in on your behalf to

deep space craft mapping
mars and jupiter
to the erratic generals with
their submerged arsenals

you're listening as if a signal
stripped from its source
rings and rings of reason

your head is so tender
the earphones drive you to migraine

the antennae pause
pointed at your every wish

**1972**
now down to one radio
and one unsteady silver
wire tacked to the side
of the house you're
face down at the desk

headphones still on a cigarette
burning out between your fingers
the lights of the receiver unblinking
tuned to the one wavelength
where you left.

# *on the shore/line*
### *la jolla, ca*

## I

the world rises with the sun / and /
the ocean folds its edge and falls /
what is known comes into view and
the ocean / folds its edge and falls

sun breaks and / light folds back the
edge / the ocean falls the light falls
/ the view unfolds / what is known
rises with the sun as the ocean folds
its edge / and falls

## II

your face follows in the water / folds
and unfolds yourself / as the sun
goes down / the shadow of the world
upon the mirror of the moon / the
light of the moon rising / your
shadow on the water / and the
mirror of the water

## III

your face follows in the water / face
of the rising moon / shadows of the
waves folding and unfolding up to the
edge of it / night after night the
moon on the waves

if you could hear it / you still could
not say it / your face with which you
face yourself / the coming and going
of the moon on the waves night after
night.

# *the inland sea*
## *sand mountain, nv*

and     still     the     waves     pile     up
. . .     the     inland     sea     in     all     its
dry     tides     . . .     blank     shoreline
buried     and     reburied     every     night
beneath     . . .     long     lines     of     sand
and     shadow     . . .

the     desert     rises     and     falls     in
the     wind     . . .     sand     folds     up     and
falls     upon     . . .     the     edge     of
the     dunes     . . .     against     the     long
division     of     basin     and     range     . . .

sand     writes     at     right     angles
to     wind     . . .     erasure     prevailing     from
west     to     east     . . .     and     in     retreat
before     the     wind     . . .     your
footsteps     . . .     over     and     over     the
shoreline     again     . . .

## II

you     rise     and     fall     over     the
dunes     . . .     walking     at     right
angles     to     the     edge     . . .     the
horizon     first     above     . . .     then
below     you     . . .     a     sentence     you
carry     out     from     the     interior     . . .
bearing     the     long     line     of     an     old
text     . . .     rolled     out     of     the     ocean
. . .

there     is     and     is     not     . . .     ocean
in     the     wind     . . .     and     still     the
waves     pile     up     . . .     meaning     long
since     evaporated     . . .     you     and     the
dunes     falling     upon     . . .     the     edge
of     all     you     read     . . .     stranded     on
a     plain     of     salt     . . .

the horizon . . . after all . . .
comes to an end . . . shoreline
disappears . . . erasure intersects
your path on an old map . . .
waves at right angles to all you
know . . . filling your footsteps
. . . one less line.

# *the island*

he opened the bottle and inside
was a piece of paper that read
. . . a message . . .

he was on of course a desert but
whether or not it was an island
he refused to decide

he opened the bottle
that came the next day
. . . the message is . . .

the waves were small and regular
just large enough to lift the bottles
. . . the next message will be . . .

he committed himself to games of solitaire
beneath the one large bush
and forgot the bottles

. . . this message is yours . . .
. . . only you know what it means . . .
. . . don't forget . . .

he kept the bottles with their messages
under the bush where he slept at night
the bottles clinking softly when he rolled over

. . . did you send this message on . . .
. . . has your fortune changed yet . . .
. . . did you hear from someone else . . .

for the first time there was a storm
all day and night huge waves
the air and ocean gray

no bottles arrived for several days but
as he slept he dreamt new messages

. . . did you forget to write . . .
. . . are you sure you are still there . . .

afterwards he climbed the low hills
and found another shore
where the waves rolled away

the next day he carried a bottle up
over the hills to the other side and
sent it on with its message

. . . any message . . .
the bottles kept coming one at a time
. . . any message will do . . .


once while playing solitaire he
read a message in the cards

. . . this is the same message . . . he read
it was the same as the one
in the bottle from the day before

at least he thought it was the same

he finished the hand and walked
down to the beach where
the next bottle was waiting

he had almost no clothes left
the water was cool on his feet
the bottle nudged his ankle

. . . keep the message and send a card . . .
the next day he did that and the next
until all the cards were gone


it was a hot day as always and he was hungry
so he decided to play solitaire with the messages
it seemed to work out

now the bottles arrived with things
inside them . . . a small fish . . .
a white cloud . . . the blue sky

were these messages too
were they words or things

he couldn't decide which so
he sent them on after taking them out
and touching them with his tongue


he caught a chill after a big storm
and then a fever came

he slept for days
bottles waiting for him
at the high tide mark

when well he didn't read the messages
but carried the bottles unopened to the other
side and they quickly receded

shortly thereafter a ship sailed by
he signaled it by flashing the sun
off the bottle that had come that day

he was rescued and kept the bottle
which he had not had time to open

like all the rest the bottle was amber
so he couldn't read the message
and he wouldn't open the bottle


one morning he got up to get the paper
at the front door was a bottle

an amber bottle so he opened it
. . . read the message . . . it said

in his study he opened his keepsake
from that time of solitaire
. . . have you forgotten . . .

he put the old bottle out the back door
and broke out a new deck

the cards rising and falling
as if caught in the waves.

# *echo*

## I

water    suspends    every    word    //    all    that
we    believe    in    a    single    trough    //    the
angular    declension    of    echo    //    many
echoes    of    the    one    wave

the    wave    itself    in    the    open    and
singular    ocean    //    carries    no    water    //
no    salt    //    no    sediment    //    but    once
and    for    all    only    the    force    of    wind    //
impressed    upon    that    various    surface

the    wind    in    the    wave    is    and    is
not    itself    //    has    pushed    the    wave    to
form    //    exhales    as    the    wave    over
reaches    itself    //    curls    and    collapses
over    and    over    //    the    one    message
never    the    same

silence expands and shrinks as // the
wave passes through // clouds of
language in its wake // air and
water suspended in what we believe //
the wave alone among its echoes //
various as the air upon the face
of the sea

## II

the    sun    rises    out    of    the    desert    //
light    and    wind    waver    at    the    edge    of
daybreak    //    the    echo    of    dawn
descending    into    //    that    wavelength    of
basin    and    range

beyond    that    evidence    of    all    we    know
and    can    think    //    if    not    speak    //    the
sun    falls    past    us    to    the    sea

first    air    then    water    //    evidence    of
echo    through    which    sound    locates    itself
//    locates    another    //    and    collides    into
language    as    the    wave    travels    on    and
on

for    a    moment    our    understanding
collapses    //    silence    expansive    //    the
standing    wave    of    the    world    drawn    out
//    a    line    beyond    calculation    //    function
of    the    one    difference    among    all
things.

# *the inland sea, again*
### *sand mountain, nv*

## III

sand    does    not    add    up   . . .   the
wind    the    water   . . .   shadows   yet
to    form   . . .   across   the   desert
floor   . . .

say    that   . . .   while   lying   on
your    back   . . .   on   top   of   the
largest    dune   . . .   sand   blowing
counterclockwise   over   you   . . .
sand    piling   up   your   left   side
and   . . .   running   out   from
underneath   your   right   . . .

say    that   you   are   there   . . .   to
count   the   clouds   . . .   all   five   of
them   almost   over   the   horizon   . . .
and   by   adding   them   . . .   wish   to
derive   the   weight   of   sunlight   . . .
at   this   end   of   the   valley   . . .

this would . . . dictate the speed
of the wind . . . the rate at
which . . . you are at once
buried and . . . undermined . . .
would recall the tide . . . where
once the waves . . . if you had
stood at the edge . . . the
folding unfolding and falling edge
. . . of the water . . .

would have undermined your
weight . . . sinking you slowly
into the shore . . . that line now
depositing along your left side . . .
feet facing the sun . . .
which sinks of its own weight
. . . behind the clouds . . .

## IV

wind    water    and    sand   . . .   do   not
yet    add    up    to   . . .   the   shadows
unfolding    here   . . .   from   the
mountains    to    the    west   . . .
behind    which    the    clouds   . . . are
now    folding    up    the    sun   . . .

wind    falls    off   . . .   you   roll
down    the    crest    of    the    dune . . .
into    its    shadow   . . .   the   cold
shadow    which    does    not    yet   . . .
add    up    to    the    edge    of   . . .   all
you    know   . . .   although    it    is
close.

# *the carrier wave*
### *janet elizabeth lyman*
### *lake powell, az*

**1971**
mother sits on the edge
of a drowned canyon
the wind and the waves
echoing up one two three
she listens to what they say
the sandstone shore eroding
one layer at a time

fifteen years in the desert
never once visiting the ocean
she sits at the edge of what she hears
waiting for what evidence the waves will
bring from that shelf of wind
off which they fall

in the dark she bears witness to
a storm that returns every night
eroding the shoreline of all she knows

runoff from the rain
silt in her veins
the erratic course of memory
gone to sea


the storm proof that
wind and water mirror everything
waves lifting birds from the water
the one motion of the many
her heart undercut over the canyon.

## ( *night writing*

between    the    waves    /    without    leaving
a    trace    /    hand    written    on    water    /
without    leaving    a    mark    /    lightning
splits    and    /    splits    the    dark

splits    perfectly    down    from    /    dark
above    to    ocean    below    /    splits    all    we
said    /    from    all    we    know    /    without
leaving    a    trace    /    from    wave    to    wave

from    ocean    to    sky    /    parallel    the
wave    /    parallel    to    the    shore    /    the
lightning    knows    /    what    we    knew    before

between    the    waves    /    with    nothing    to
say    /    written    on    water    /    and    split
away    /    parallel    from    the    rest    /
parallel    to    the    shore    /    lightning    splits
off    /    what    we    said    before    ).

## *the function of divorce*
### *santa barbara, ca / reno, nv*

**I**
listen
you must write letters
letters about the cracks
which separate the walls

you must
listen to the cracks and
write down the letters
which appear

you should appear to be
listening at the cracks

write letters to me every
day of the cracks between
the east wall of our
understanding and the west
wall of our misfortune

the house of our lives our
two lives falling away in
what seems to be the
letter of the law

## II

you must watch how the stars
reconfigure the dark
how the moon lights up
what you write

sign off every letter as if
you could picture
what you are saying
the airport beacon
sweeping over the crickets
its green and white lights
a signal from the past

think of that beacon
how what you write
sweeps clear the page each night

**III**

don't take for granted
that you can letter each
star in an atlas and
catalog what you hear

and don't forget the slate roof
wiped clean by rain last night
the switch of the constellations
flicked off before morning
the letter by the bed
finished

listen
the night too
cracks at dawn and all
must be written down beforehand

**IV**
it's that wind again
your mother crying
on a bridge after the war
pulling that wind through her

wedding ring a lullaby wrung from
mother to daughter

nothing had been lost yet
her husband safe her
daughter to be born
but she knew she'd throw herself away

in that wind years later the airport
beacon sweeping before her

her husband dead the daughter
gone the lullaby come again
letters falling out of the cracks
between walls

## V

no code is more difficult
than the crickets'
that ragged graph of humidity
the iteration of luna
in a mating cycle

you say it's simple to
reproduce it on tape to
display the interval the frequency
the oscillation of sex on a
computer screen but listen

can you stand in the dark at the
screen door and count the crickets
measure their distance from each other
and the throw weight of their desire
by listening

can you recall the
date they started the
date they ended  last year

the number of strokes per
second at which they
captured your attention

## VI.

finally it's obvious
the crickets in the
cracks of the house
falling down at the edge
of the airfield

the beacon and your hand
sweeping clear the runway of
the past for what might appear

the wind tunes up for that
lullaby of loss your mother
wrung out of her fingers
all those years ago and now
it's you listening and
writing it down

and if you can't estimate
what the crickets and the stars
choreograph between themselves
there is the act of listening

of writing this letter
of getting the crack
out of which it all falls
just right
in the middle of the page.

# the carrier wave

**1958**
from outside the breaking waves i'm
waving at the shoreline and the line of hills
waving at our house above the shore

and at my mother who rises up then
falls back out of sight as i
fall between clear swells

i'm rising and falling in place
with the lift of her arm from shore
never far from what i know

that the horizon behind my back
is flat and incomplete
that father is in the house
rising and falling on the airwaves
of his own choice

no words from wave to shore
from shore to house
mother's arm rising and falling

**1966**
the edge of the ocean rises
then falls away as i wait for
the last wave of the day

a long ride to shore where a window
in just one instant
has blinked into mirror

time rises and falls away
in that wavering glass
sun setting through the breaking
wave of family

the ocean gone black from
shore to horizon
every wave beneath me
a chance to go home

for now
outside that invisible break
only the sound of waves
between here and there

the decay of signal from
mother to father to son

lights ashore rising and
falling in the night

**1986**
red aces lift and drop in the desert
far beyond any break
and fortune decays

father has been lifted from his desk
mother lifted from her bed
both blown feet first into ash

and the arm of the dealer lifts
then lets fall card after card

the horizon is a sentence i live out
from edge to incomplete edge
what i level against the world as a child

desiring nothing more than to
step over that line and not look back

now i justify the margins
the sea and the desert against
the end of what we know
and where begins what we don't.

# the island, again

his house is on a hill
the ocean so far below
he cannot hear the waves

he does not expect words
in a bottle anymore

does not anticipate the
arrival of anyone else

just the fog every night and
someday the message

the wave that will
pass through him


he walks the crest
of the hill for miles

changing the angle at which
he views the sea and the
open spine of the horizon

at night he dreams of solitaire
on what was perhaps an island

of his rescue and relocation
the worn pack of cards left
neatly played out on his desk

a perfect hand unopened
on the shore of all he knew

and now he furrows the hill
deaf from solitude

this will not save him
the message will arrive and

again put him in the middle
of a sentence he cannot escape.

# *horizon*

a   stranger   looks   over   your   shoulder   /
low   hill   of   dusk   behind   you   /   the
knot   of   language   undone   /   contents   at
odd   with   each   other   /   and   with   you
/   specifically   you   /   the   one   writing
down   these   words   /   that   you   cannot
use   again

far   below   /   sand   and   water   stand   in
waves   /   the   ratio   of   horizon   to   sky   /
one   line   to   a   page   /   and   in   that
line   the   signature   of   a   wave   /   as   it
leaves   what   is   written

between   incoming   words   /   and
outgoing   lines   /   between   what   you   see
and   cannot   hear   /   wind   on   the   water
pushes   it   all   ashore   /   words   breaking
up   on   the   page   /   meaning   run
aground

behind you the dark hill advances /
desert of the page stretched as far
as we can speak / the edge of the
word at the end of the land

how you / who are writing / stand
above the sea / divide the lines one
from another / the interval of each
wave identical / gray air / white
noise

waves fall in line / betray nothing of
what will be said / bring no message
from the horizon beyond which words
amass / thunderclouds of the unspoken.

# *receiving*

in this inversion of the wave // glass
// the standing still point of sand and
wind // open face of the ocean held
up to light // the face of our lives
held in the wave // the passing of
time

through that window upstairs // as
transparent as open air // our lives
rise and fall in the glass by the
bed // water trembling // curtains
blowing across the room

i look through that window to the
figure of my father // on the other
side of that glass which separates us
from what we say // one-way mirror
through which the past // and from
which the future // remain always on
the other side

the wave of time lifts us up //
then lets us fall on that other side
// father waving into the mirror //
our future suspended in language //
the one transparent wave of the
world.

## *the message...*
### *very large array, nm*

.  .  .    was    never    the    tree    and
the    hieroglyph    it    inscribed    outside
the    window    .  .  .    never    the    books
and    how    they    whistled    as    they
fell    one    against    another    in    the
bookshelf    .  .  .    never    the    arc
tortured    out    of    the    sky    by    birds
and    pinned    to    either    side    of
town    .  .  .    neither  ·  geometry    nor
a    figure    of    speech    .  .  .    was
never    the    reflection    of    your
shadow    in    the    mirror    and    how
it    traversed    to    another    shadow
just    out    of    sight    .  .  .

.  .  .    nor    the    singular    column    of
snowflakes    that    appeared    on    the
windowsill    .  .  .    nor    the    uneven
number    of    knots    woven    all
along    the    branch    by    that    wind

from     the     south     that     left     all     the
dust     lined     up     as     long     division
.  .  .     never     the     fence     the
alternating     grain     of     the     wood
with     its     grimaces  .  .  .

        .  .  .     was     never     the     fourth     leg
of     the     kitchen     table  .  .  .     the
almost     coherent     tattoo     it     would
beat     out     quietly     during     dinner     as
everyone     shifted     their     plates  .  .  .     never
the     corner     of     the     rug     in
the     upstairs     guest     room     turning
up     to     reveal     the     tattletale
nailheads  .  .  .     never     the     clouds
with     their     intricate     plots     to
eradicate     the     constellations  .  .  .

        .  .  .     nor     were     the     iron     rail     ties
dancing     on     their     long     bed     under
the     weight     of     all     our     goods     the
message  .  .  .     the     truth     the
whole     story     or     anything

resembling    our    lives    .  .  .    no
matter    how    much    it    all    looked
and    sounded    like    the    language
we    had    lost    just    as    we    learned
to    speak.

*colophon*

Set in **Sabon**—
Jan Tschichold's modern version of
*Garamond*, specifically designed for the
(then) requirements of mechanical
composition. Named after *Jacques Sabon*,
a punchcutter from Lyons who brought
the original matrices of Claude Garamond
to Frankfurt, this typeface represents
Tschichold's synthesis of practicability
and fundamental elegance.

•

*Book design by J. Bryan*

William L. Fox was born in San Diego in 1949 and moved to Reno ten years later. Living in California, Nevada, and New Mexico, he has circumnavigated the Basin and Range province of the West as an editor and publisher with various literary magazines and presses since 1969. His previous publications include thirteen collections of poems, several exhibition catalogs, and two books of essays on the relationships between art and land. He currently resides in Los Angeles.

### Poetry Books/Chapbooks

*two canyons*, 1997

*silence*, 1995

*geograph*, 1994

*leaving elko*, 1993

*Reliquaire*, 1988

*Time by Distance*, 1985

*21 and Over*, 1982

*The Yellow Pages*, 1980

*First Principles*, 1978

*Monody*, 1977

*Election*, 1973

*Trial Separation*, 1972

*Iron Wind*, 1971